The Farndale Avenue Housing Estate Townswomen's Guild Dramatic Society Murder Mystery

A Comedy
(Revised version)

David McGillivray
and
Walter Zerlin Jnr

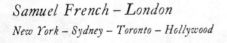

Samuel French – London
New York – Sydney – Toronto – Hollywood

© 1981 by The Entertainment Machine Theatre Co Ltd

1. *This play is fully protected under the Copyright Laws of the British Commonwealth of Nations, the United States of America and all countries of the Berne and Universal Copyright Conventions.*

2. *All rights, including Stage, Motion Picture, Radio, Television, Public Reading and Translation into Foreign Languages, are strictly reserved.*

3. **No part of this publication may lawfully be reproduced in ANY form or by any means—photocopying, typescript, recording (including video-recording), manuscript, electronic, mechanical, or otherwise—or be transmitted or stored in a retrieval system, without prior permission.**

4. Rights of Performance by Amateurs are controlled by Samuel French Ltd, 52 Fitzroy Street, London W1P 6JR, and they, or their authorized agents, issue licences to amateurs to give performances of this play on payment of a fee. **It is an infringement of the Copyright to give any performance or public reading of the play before the fee has been paid and the licence issued.**

5. Licences are issued subject to the understanding that it shall be made clear in all advertising matter that the audience will witness an amateur performance; that the names of the authors of the plays shall be included on all announcements and on all programmes; and that the integrity of the author's work will be preserved.

The Royalty Fee indicated below is subject to contract and subject to variation at the sole discretion of Samuel French Ltd.

> Basic fee for each and every
> performance by amateurs   Code L
> in the British Isles

In Theatres or Halls seating Six Hundred or more the fee will be subject to negotiation.

In Territories Overseas the fee quoted above may not apply. A fee will be quoted on application to our local authorized agent, or if there is no such agent, on application to Samuel French Ltd, London.

The publication of this play does not imply that it is necessarily available for performance by amateurs or professionals, either in the British Isles or Overseas. Amateurs and professionals considering a production are strongly advised in their own interests to apply to the appropriate agents for consent before starting rehearsals or booking a theatre or hall.

ISBN 0 573 11141 3

THE FARNDALE AVENUE HOUSING ESTATE
TOWNSWOMEN'S GUILD DRAMATIC SOCIETY
MURDER MYSTERY

First produced at the Edinburgh Festival Fringe on August 18th, 1980, with the following cast of characters:

Sylvia (playing **Inspector O'Reilly**)	Pippa Sparkes
Felicity (playing **Pawn**, a butler; **Colonel King**, Lady Bishop's brother-in-law)	Philomena McDonagh
Audrey (playing **Lady Doreen Bishop**, a widow; **Violet Bishop**, her spinster aunt; **Mrs King**, the Colonel's wife; **Joan Bishop**, Lady Bishop's cousin)	Anne-Marie Davies
Mrs Reece (playing **Clarissa Rook**, Lady Bishop's sister; **Régine**, the French maid; **Patricia Bishop**, Lady Bishop's niece; **Letitia Bishop**, her sister; **Mr Goodbody**, a solicitor)	Louise Barclay
Thelma (playing **Daphne Bishop**, Lady Bishop's daughter; **Rose Bishop**, her spinster aunt)	Jeannie May Selfe
The Producer	David McGillivray

Directed by David McGillivray
Designed by Walter Zerlin Jnr and Gerald Tagg

This revised version was first produced at the Swan Theatre, Stratford-upon-Avon on March 14th, 1988, with the following cast of characters:

Gordon (playing **Inspector O'Reilly**)	David McGillivray
Felicity	Mary Roscoe
Audrey	Angela Moran
Mrs Reece	Marie Collett
Thelma	Jean Selfe

Directed by David McGillivray
Designed by Walter Zerlin Jnr and Gerald Tagg

AUTHORS' NOTE

Whenever a Dramatic Society has told us that they're about to perform their version of *The Farndale/Murder Mystery*, we've asked them to hold everything while we rushed them a new manuscript version of the play containing the latest in a long series of revisions. What a relief to all concerned that our publishers have now consented to issue a second edition, complete with every alteration and additional piece of business, little and large, invented during four professional productions of *The Farndale/Murder Mystery* staged since it was first published in 1981. Sylvia has had a sex change because we found the audience preferred the contrasts offered by a mixed cast. We've removed an inchoate piece of suitcase business we later brought to fruition in *The Haunted Through Lounge* ... We've also taken the opportunity to describe precisely the chair-moving routine in Act II. We hope you agree that the changes are improvements, and we promise to do no further rewriting.

David McGillivray
Walter Zerlin Jnr
London, April 1988

PROLOGUE

On stage there is a scene representing the drawing-room on the second floor of Checkmate Manor, Lady Doreen Bishop's ancestral home, an isolated house near the sea. Leading off R is a staircase. Below this is a painted door. There is an exit through a curtained archway UL. Practical windows UC, and through them a view of rolling hills on a summer's day. A fireplace R of the windows with a portrait of The Laughing Cavalier *hanging on the same flat. Furniture includes a large armchair C, a table bearing a chess-board and pieces DR and a standard lamp UL. At the front of the auditorium is a home movie screen and 8mm projector*

Mrs Reece, chairman of the Dramatic Society, and her second-in-command Thelma, who is wearing a sash reading "Miss Farndale 1988", are on hand to welcome the audience and settle them into their seats. The ladies sell programmes, each one containing a slip of paper to be used for the Murder Mystery Quiz, and give away samples of Mrs Dabney's home-made fudge

Five minutes before the advertised start of the play, the scenery disintegrates. First the painting comes off the fireplace flat. Then the pelmet and curtains fall off the window flat. The leg comes off the chess-table sending the board and pieces all over the floor. Finally the fireplace flat falls on to the stage

Felicity and Audrey appear and replace the flat back-to-front, revealing pieces of paper with people's cues written on them stuck to the other side. They are about to exit when they realize their mistake. They turn the flat the correct way round, then exit not realizing that it is now upside-down

Pre-show music ends with a fanfare. In the ensuing silence Mrs Reece can be heard arguing with Thelma. They break off and come down to the front of the auditorium

Mrs Reece Caught me on the hop. Sorry. Just one or two announcements before we begin: first of all some of you may have heard that we had a little calamity last night with the interval teas. Now we haven't as yet found out exactly who it was who misbehaved themselves in the tea urn. But we have spent all day scrubbing the thing out with Dettol. And I can assure you that there's nothing wrong with the water tonight. I passed it myself. Also I'd like to draw your attention to a change in the programme. The part of Inspector O'Reilly will not be played by Sylvia Frobisher. As you know Sylvia's not that quick on her feet, and that floodlight really did fetch her a heck of a thump on the head. But I spoke to her *au pair* this morning and apparently Sylvia has started forming sentences. Which is more than she could do when she was in the play. But with any luck she'll be up and about for the dinner dance. And stepping into the breach tonight is our stage manager Gordon Pugh. I know we're going to be behind him tonight because he hasn't acted since he played the second ox in *The Star of Bethlehem*. And finally those of you who were at this year's AGM will know that we had to cancel the traditional screening of Mrs Beasley's holiday movies due to the controversy surrounding the election of "Miss Farndale", an incident I won't elaborate on now because we don't want to open old sores. Suffice it to say that the title went *eventually* to Thelma Greenwood, our perennial leading lady. And perennial Miss Farndale. And I'm sure we all admire her diligence in demanding fourteen recounts. Even if it did mean missing the movie. Which Mrs Beasley had brought in specially. At great cost. And she doesn't get much out of life. It's not as if she's a well woman ...

Thelma We're pushing against time here, Phoebe.

Mrs Reece (*to Thelma*) Really? (*To the audience*) She's not at all well. Although I'm sure you'll all be pleased to hear the cartilage operation was a success. So now we're going to see Mrs Beasley's latest production. In Super Beasley-Vision. "Hello, Isle of Man." All right, Thelma.

House Lights down. Thelma switches on the projector and projects an out-of-focus picture that is an eighth on the screen and seven-eighths on the wall. Mrs Reece is reading from notes and doesn't notice

The first thing you'll see is a shot of Douglas taken in early morning sunlight from the ferry. These people in oilskins are a couple the Beasleys met on board. And the lady is a member of the Stourbridge Towns-women's Guild. Isn't that a coincidence? (*She looks at the screen. To Thelma*) I think it could do with a little shift to the starboard side, dear.

Thelma jerks the projector about trying to centre the picture

That's the harbour just flashing past there. (*To Thelma*) Back to where you were, dear. That's perfect.

The picture is so out of focus that absolutely nothing is distinguishable

I think this is the House of Keys. No, it's the Beasleys' hotel, and there's Mrs Beasley's husband pointing up at their suite. Can you see him? Hasn't he lost weight? Quite a super-slimmer. Where are we now? I think this is the new oil refinery at Rue Point. Seen through fog probably. The weather is so unpredictable over there, isn't it? I was over there a few years ago for their Jubilee or whatever it was, and one never knew ... There's a Manx cat! Oh, it's gone. But there are the scratch marks on Mr Beasley's leg. Isn't that wonderful?

The film suddenly breaks leaving a glaring white screen

Was that meant to happen?

Thelma Anyone got some Sellotape?

The House Lights come up

Thelma exits

Mrs Reece Evidently not. You know, ladies and gentlemen, this may sound foolish, but I sometimes think our productions are jinxed. I do. I mean, I've been out and about. I've been to the Old Vic and Stratford-upon-Avon. Nothing goes wrong with their shows. Of course they're not as adventurous as us. I suppose you can't have everything. (*She looks towards the wings*) Any joy with the Sellotape, people?

General cries of woe from backstage

Hmmmm. Well, I'm afraid we may have to draw a veil over this débâcle. But we saw most of the best bits. So let's get on with our little play. And do concentrate like mad, won't you, because we're going to have a competition later on to see how eagle-eyed you've been.

Felicity appears

Felicity Henry says will chewing gum do?
Mrs Reece No, we're not bothering, dear. Is everyone ready back here?

They exit. Audrey wanders casually on stage, takes out a cigarette, lights it, sits down, picks up a magazine and opens it. Her expression changes to surprise

Audrey Sorry. Have we started?

She runs off

The House Lights go down

ACT I

The drawing-room of Checkmate Manor. It is a winter evening

There is a thunder and lightning effect strangely at odds with the bright sunlight coming through the window. Mrs Reece, as Clarissa, can be seen running across the stage from L to R, struggling into a nightgown. As soon as she has climbed the stairs to the top, the Lights come up, revealing Clarissa buttoning her nightgown and waiting for her cue. There is a knocking, off. Clarissa remembers something she has forgotten, gestures into the wings and is handed a piano accordion

Clarissa No, that's later.

She is handed a candlestick instead. She descends the stairs

Humph. Three o'clock in the morning is a fine time for somebody to be calling at my sister Doreen's remote country house by the sea.

More knocking

I suppose I'd better find out who it is. If only I could find the light switch so I could illuminate my way down the stairs. Ah, here it is. Brrrr, what a terrible ... (*She clicks the switch on the window flat*)

Black-out

They're supposed to be on now.

The Lights come up full suddenly. Clarissa tries to validate this cue by flicking the switch again. Imperfect Black-out

No, I want them on! One—two—three.

This allows the electrician to synchronize. Clarissa flicks the switch and the Lights come up full

(*Looking out of the window*) Brrrr, what a terrible night. Just look at that snow.

Snow flutters down the inside of the window much to the surprise of Clarissa, who jumps away confused

She hurries off R

More knocking

(*Off*) I'm coming, I'm coming. Oh, it's you, is it? Forgot your keys again, I suppose. I should have gone off the other side, shouldn't I? Oh, fiddle.

Clarissa enters and runs across stage from R *to* L

Won't be a jiff.

She exits L

(*Off*) Sorry, I'm not thinking. Oh, it's you, is it? Forgot your keys again, I suppose.

Clarissa enters L *and stands with her back to the arch*

Do you realize that since I arrived here you've knocked me up three times? You'll have to be more careful in future.

Felicity's white-gloved hands stretch out from the arch towards Clarissa's neck

After all, it would be the absolute living end if my sister learned of our intricately devised plot. So we're going to have to be frightfully secretive in the future, I can tell you.

The hands, unable to reach their target, make little beckoning movements

Well, why are you just standing there behind me? Haven't you got anything to say for yourself?

Felicity (*stage whisper from the wings*) Yes, move back! I can't reach you.

Clarissa realizes and leans back so that she can be strangled. As soon as the hands touch her throat she begins struggling violently

> *In the struggle Felicity, as Pawn the butler, is pulled from the wings and seen quite plainly. She forgets about the throttling and darts back out of sight*

Clarissa notices her absence and strangles herself, folding up on the floor. There is an imperfect Black-out during which Clarissa can be seen to get up, hurry to the window and pick up the pelmet and curtains. The Lights come up revealing her replacing them

Clarissa Drat!

> *She exits* L *as Audrey, playing Lady Doreen Bishop, enters down the stairs and screams. She walks uncertainly to the spot where Clarissa's body isn't and studies the empty space*

Doreen Clarissa!

Clarissa creeps in R, *clutching a chess-piece, and lies on the floor*

Doreen moves to the bell-rope L *and, as she pulls it, it comes away in her hand*

> *Pawn enters* L

Doreen hands Pawn the bell-rope and he throws it through the curtains of the arch

Pawn You rang, milady?

Doreen Ah, Pawn. Come here quickly, man. Something utterly ghastly has happened to my sister, Clarissa, who, as you can see, is lying here at my feet.

Pawn realizes the true position of Clarissa and pushes Doreen in the appropriate direction

Pawn Grip yourself, ma'am. It's strangulation what we have here.
Doreen You mean she's dead?
Pawn Alack, that is the case.

Clarissa has a coughing fit

Doreen Poor Clarissa. And on a wonderful day like today.
Pawn What a tragedy.
Doreen Is that a lifeless chess-piece I see clutched in Clarissa's black hand?
Pawn Yes, a bishop.
Doreen But Bishop is our family name. Could there be a connection?
Pawn Not half, milady. Look at this here chess-board.

They move to where the chess-pieces are scattered over the floor

Doreen Why, yes, this is as clear as day. A black bishop is missing from the board.
Pawn Snort. Well, there is nothing we can do to solve this mystery. Shall I telephone for the police?
Doreen Be so good as to do that.

Pawn discovers he doesn't know where the telephone is and enquires into both wings without success

Pawn (*consulting the "corpse"*) Have you seen the telephone, Mrs Reece?
Clarissa Underneath the chair, dear.

Pawn removes the telephone from underneath the armchair, and places it on the table

Doreen (*ad libbing*) How's that telephone call coming along, Pawn?
Pawn Just trying to get through, milady.

He picks up the receiver and speaks into it without pausing at all during the speech. Simultaneously Doreen reconstructs the chess-table, and is handed a dustpan and brush from off stage with which she sweeps up the chess-pieces

(*On the phone*) Good-morning. This is Pawn, Lady Bushop's bitler at Checkmate Manor. Yes, it is indeed a capital morning, but I fear we must discuss a graver matter than—oh. (*He replaces the receiver, picks it up again and dials a number and speaks without pausing as before*) Good-morning. This is Pawn, Lady Butler's bishop at Checkmate Manor. Yes, it is indeed a capital morning, but I fear we must discuss a graver matter than the weather. What am I driving at? I'll tell you, Officer. Murder that's what. (*He takes the receiver, looks at it quizzically, and then replaces it to his ear*) No, this is not a practical joke. There is a corpse up here and it smells fishy to me. What's that you say? The inspector will make this case a priority? I'll inform her ladyship. (*He hangs up. To Doreen*) Good news . . . (*He picks up the receiver again*) Thank you very much. Goodbye. (*He hangs up again. To Doreen*) Good news, your lady . . . m'ship shape lady . . . Inspector O'Reilly will be here in a flash.

Doreen disposes of the chess-pieces by tipping them on to the chess-board

Doreen O'Reilly? But he's the man who solved the Limehouse murders. Tell Régine, our French maid, to take the plastic covers off the armchairs and put an extra coat of liquid Gumption on the wash basin in the guest cloakroom.

Pawn I hasten to do your bidding, ma'am.

Thelma, as Daphne in a tennis outfit, makes false entrance L and then retreats off

Doreen Hold your horses, though. Do you hear a faint scuffling outside the door?

Pawn A faint scuffling? Why, no.

Doreen Surely my ears do not deceive me. Hist.

Deafening sound as of several flats falling to the ground

Voice (*off*) You blithering idiot!

Pawn The house is as silent as the grave, milady.

Doreen It would certainly seem so. And yet some sixth sense warns me we are not alone.

Pawn Is someone out there trying to put the wind up milady?

Daphne (*off*) It is only I, dear Pawn.

Doreen Phew! We were becoming agitated by none other than my own daughter, Daphne.

Pawn The enchanting lass.

He and Doreen face in opposite directions to greet Daphne

Doreen (*beckoning into the wings*) Daphne, darling . . .

After some moments Thelma, as Daphne, bounds in, holding a tennis racquet and ball. She opens and closes her mouth and flaps her tennis racquet about—she has forgotten her lines

Doreen and Pawn dart their eyes at each other nervously. Suddenly Daphne panics, screams and falls on top of Clarissa, causing her to groan in pain

She's going to faint. Quick, Pawn, catch her.

Pawn She's safe in my grasp, milady.

They move to Doreen, crouching by her side

Doreen This has been too much of a shock for her teenage metabolism. Thank goodness I always carry smelling salts with me. (*She fumbles for the smelling-salts she's forgotten. To Pawn*) Would you administer them?

Pawn Where are they?

Doreen Haven't got them.

Daphne surreptitiously produces them from her pocket and hands them to Pawn

Daphne, darling, speak to your mother.

Daphne Mother, I've just had the most terrible dream. I thought I saw Aunt
Clarissa lying dead.

Doreen It was no dream, darling. Clarissa has passed on violently.

Daphne You mean she blabbed and someone rubbed her out? (*She gets up*)

Doreen Where do you pick up these crude expressions? Pawn, kindly
remove my sister in a dignified fashion.

Pawn I am, ma'am, your obedient servant.

Doreen Daphne, now that we're alone . . . (*She hands dustpan and brush to
Clarissa*) Take that off for me, Phoebe.

*Pawn takes hold of Clarissa's feet, pulls, and removes her shoes. He and
Clarissa struggle off* R, *all the time within easy earshot of the following:*

Daphne, now that we're alone, I must chastise you for making irrespon-
sible remarks about Clarissa in front of faithful old Pawn.

Daphne But, Mother, even old Pawn knew that Aunt Clarissa was one of
several members of our family who were involved in a conspiracy to
discover the contents of Daddy's will, which is being read tomorrow
evening.

*Daphne uses her racquet to bounce the tennis ball on the floor, but it bounces
away and she loses it. Another ball is bounced on from the wings and she uses
this instead before losing it. A succession of balls—some of different colours—
appears, much to Daphne's annoyance*

Doreen I must admit that you are correct on two counts, Daphne. Firstly
your aunt was indeed a mercenary woman whose cravings overstepped
the bounds of decency. Equally, her desire to have your late father's will
altered in her favour was an open secret.

*She stops and stares in astonishment at the tennis balls bouncing round her.
They cease*

This means, of course, that practically everyone in our household had a
motive to kill her. Come in.

Pause. Nothing happens

*Mrs Reece, now dressed as Régine the French maid, is seen running behind
the window,* L *to* R

There is knocking, off

Come in.

*Régine enters with a tray and bad French accent. She adjusts her uniform,
steps forward and the cap comes off*

Régine Bonjour, madame. I am the French maid now, aren't I?

Doreen Yes. What is it, Régine?

Régine I 'ave prepared ze 'ouse as you wish, madame. Shall I now boil ze
doilies in ze room of Mamzelle Clarissa?

Doreen No. Miss Rook will no longer require her boilies doiled on account
of her being dead.

Régine (*dropping the tray*) Mon Dieu!
Doreen You foolish girl. Those stains will now have to be soaked in a solution of vinegar and warm soapy water. And what a time for such a thing to happen. I can hear Inspector O'Reilly's police car approaching.

There is the sound effect of vast traffic noise: horns blowing, juggernauts changing gear, newsvendors' cries, etc. Eventually a police siren emerges from the mêlée, then the entire effect stops abruptly. There is a knocking, off

Pawn enters L

Pawn Inspector O'Reilly, milady.
Doreen Ah, Pawn, who is it?
Pawn Inspector O'Reilly, milady.
Doreen Good. Show him in.

Pawn bows, steps backwards and treads on the foot of Gordon, playing Inspector O'Reilly, who enters behind him. He is wearing a trenchcoat

O'Reilly Ow!

There is confusion as Pawn makes a hasty exit

Lady Bishop?
Doreen Yes, I've been inspecting you, Expector. Come in and warm yourself by the fire.
O'Reilly My, what a grand blaze. (*He notices with surprise the upside down flat and stretches his hands upwards to warm them*)
Doreen Yes, so welcoming, don't you think? Régine, a glass of sherry for our guest.
Régine Not yet.
Doreen Oh, sorry. Em . . . may I introduce my daughter Daphne?
O'Reilly With the greatest of pleasure.
Daphne How do you do, Inspector.
Doreen And would you care for a glass of sherry?
O'Reilly Well, just a soupçon.
Doreen Régine, a glass of sherry for our guest.
Régine Oui, madame.

Régine curtsies and exits L

O'Reilly moves up R. *Doreen sits in the armchair*

O'Reilly I'm sorry we have to meet under such unfortunate circumstances, milady.
Doreen Ah, yes. Clarissa was too, too young. I expect you'll want to inspect her, Inspector?
O'Reilly I fear that will be my hapless duty. But first I must make some notes. What can you tell me about . . . (*he forgets the name*) . . . your sister.
Doreen She was my sister. (*She picks up the sewing box. The bottom falls out and everything is left on the floor. She extricates her embroidery and begins sewing on her lap, attaching it to her dress*) She had recently arrived here at Checkmate Manor for the reading of my late husband's will.

O'Reilly Might I say, milady, that your late husband, Sir Reginald Bishop, was a fine man.

Régine enters L with what is obviously a glass of orange juice. Seeing that O'Reilly is up R, she exits

Doreen A fine man? Why, yes, some might think so. But those of us who lived with him knew better.

O'Reilly Be so good as to elaborate.

Daphne My father was little more than an animal, Inspector. No, Mother, let me speak. Don't interrupt me, please, Mother. You know he would use Brillo pads on the Teflon saucepans and refuse to walk on newspapers after the kitchen floor had been washed.

O'Reilly moves down R

O'Reilly How did you tolerate such behaviour, Lady Bishop?

Régine enters up R and exits when she sees O'Reilly has moved again

Doreen Look around you, Inspector. I had everything a woman could desire. Reggie may have been a pig, but at least he was well-endowed. Another sherry?

O'Reilly No. But may I compliment you on the rich, red ruby nectar I have in my hand?

He turns as we hear bumping behind the DR door

Régine (*off*) Door won't open.

O'Reilly crosses to the door and makes an abortive attempt to grasp a non-existent handle

O'Reilly It's not a real door.

Régine (*off*) Sugar.

O'Reilly Have you got the rich, red ruby nectar?

The orange juice is passed round the top of the stairs

Doreen I like a man who appreciates a fine, dry Cyprus. Hold it up to the light, Inspector.

O'Reilly raises the glass too sharply, sending a spout of orange juice shooting into the air. As it descends, he attempts to catch it in the glass again. Doreen sees this spectacle. She and O'Reilly make the mistake of looking at each other. They go into surreptitious spasms of laughter, O'Reilly turning his back to the audience, and Doreen burying her face in her bosom. Daphne clears her throat loudly and pointedly. Doreen and O'Reilly recover themselves

See how ...

Doreen and O'Reilly begin giggling again

Daphne (*furious*) Stop it.

Doreen See how ...

More corpsing

Daphne Pull yourselves together!
Doreen (*doing so*) See how its warm texture seems to emit a friendly glow.
O'Reilly It is divine.

There is a long pause with more suppressed giggling. Daphne seethes

Daphne Are there any more questions you wish to ask us, *Inspector*?
O'Reilly (*subsiding*) Most certainly.

*He places the glass of orange juice on the chess-table, which collapses again.
This sends Doreen and O'Reilly into further paroxysms*

*O'Reilly leaves the stage entirely for a couple of moments, then returns with
a terribly straight face*

(*Addressing the floor*) I shall have to interview everyone who was in the
house at the time of the crime.
Doreen The only people you have not yet met are my two spinster aunts,
Rose and Violet Bishop, who are asleep upstairs.
O'Reilly Where are they?
Doreen They're asleep upstairs.

Pawn enters L

Pawn Dinner is served, milady.

A gong is heard, off

Doreen Will you join us, Inspector?
O'Reilly You are most gracious, ma'am.

*Doreen rises, tries to remove embroidery from her lap and realizes she has
sewn it to her dress. To avoid another outburst, she starts to go out* L

Doreen (*as she goes*) Perhaps you'll be so good as to accompany my
daughter?

*O'Reilly nods, trying to conceal his laughter. Daphne moves to him and grips
him violently by the arm*

Doreen exits

Daphne What strong, powerful arms you have, Inspector.

Régine enters L

Régine Please, Inspectair, I must speak wiz you.
Pawn Régine! Be about your business, my girl.

A dog barks, off

Down, boy

Black-out

Pawn, O'Reilly and Daphne exit

The Lights come up again revealing Régine trying to repair the chess-table

Daphne enters, dabbing her lips with a napkin

Daphne (*to Régine*) Get off. (*Into the wings*) Come on!

Régine exits. O'Reilly enters L, minus trenchcoat, also dabbing his lips with a napkin

O'Reilly What a positively delightful meal, Thelma . . . Daphne.

Daphne It was nothing.

O'Reilly But what about that delicious lemon soufflé, which added a touch of sheer luxury to the bill of fare?

Daphne Well, it may have seemed ultra-sophisticated, but in fact it's so quick and easy to prepare.

O'Reilly I must make a note of the recipe.

Daphne Let me see if I can remember it. Ah, yes. To serve six to eight people put the yolks of four eggs, five ounces of sugar, half a pint of water, half an ounce of gelatine, and the grated rind of two lemons into a large basin.

O'Reilly Will a wash-basin do?

Daphne Certainly not. Then put the basin over a saucepan of hot water and whisk the mixture until it's light and creamy. Remove from the heat and add the juice of two lemons and continue to whisk until thick. Add half a pint of double cream and the whisked egg whites. Turn this into a soufflé dish and leave to set. Decorate with whipped cream and nuts.

O'Reilly Mmmmm, thanks, Daphne. I'm sure the boys at the station will want to give this to their wives tonight.

Daphne And what about you, Inspector? Will you be giving it to your wife tonight?

O'Reilly I would if I had one. But, truth to tell, I'm fancy free. What about you?

Daphne As free as air, although . . .

O'Reilly What?

Daphne It doesn't matter.

O'Reilly Tell me.

Daphne No.

O'Reilly Why?

Daphne It still hurts.

O'Reilly What does?

Daphne The pain.

O'Reilly Of losing?

Daphne Yes.

O'Reilly Who?

Daphne Randolph.

O'Reilly Were you . . . ?

Daphne Yes.

O'Reilly What happened?

Daphne It doesn't matter.

O'Reilly Tell me.

Daphne No.

O'Reilly Why?

Daphne It still hurts.

Pause

O'Reilly The pain.
Daphne Yes. Of losing.
O'Reilly Randolph.
Daphne Yes.
O'Reilly And you were ... ?
Daphne Yes.
O'Reilly What happened?
Daphne It doesn't matter.
O'Reilly Tell me.
Daphne No.
O'Reilly Why?

Long pause

Daphne It still hurts.

Longer pause

O'Reilly I see. The pain still hurts.
Daphne Yes. Of losing Randolph.
O'Reilly And you were ... ?
Daphne Yes! We were!
O'Reilly (*desperately*) What happened?
Daphne (*desperately*) It doesn't matter.
O'Reilly Tell me.
Daphne No.
O'Reilly Why?

Panic-stricken pause

Daphne It still hurts.
O'Reilly So the pain of losing Randolph still——
Daphne No, Inspector. Tell me something about yourself.
O'Reilly (*horrified, finally*) I'm fancy free although ...
Daphne What?
O'Reilly It doesn't matter.
Daphne Tell me.
O'Reilly No.
Daphne Why?
O'Reilly (*through laughter*) It still hurts.

Régine enters R *with a feather duster*

Régine Excuse-moi, monsieur. I 'ave made up a spare room for you in ze bed.
O'Reilly Thank you, Régine. Daphne—I'm glad you told me everything.
Daphne So am I, Inspector. Good-night.

Daphne skips off R

Régine (*running down to O'Reilly*) Inspectair, Inspectair, I 'ave vital information for you about ze killer of Mamzelle Clarissa.

O'Reilly Well? Spit it out, girl.

Pawn sidles on R carrying a tray with a bottle and glasses stuck to it. When he realizes he's being observed by Régine, he drops the tray by his side and goes upstairs, dislodging the banister

Régine No, I cannot speak now. Meet me 'ere at midnight. If you want a little bedtime reading, Inspector, you will find a très interesting book behind you. Bonsoir.

Régine exits R

O'Reilly looks in vain behind him. There are no books. Eventually the window opens and a subtle attempt is made to pass the book through. This fails to attract his attention and the book is hurled at him

O'Reilly (*picking up the book and looking at the cover*) Hmmmmm. *Advanced Chess*. (*He opens the book*) "Chapter One. How to Annihilate The Opposition In Nine Moves." Nine moves . . .

Joan (*off*) Hello there! Anyone about up here?

O'Reilly puts the book on one of the U chairs

O'Reilly Who is that?

Audrey, as Joan Bishop, an archaeologist in spectacles and tweeds, enters L with two obviously empty red suitcases

My name is Inspector O'Reilly. Are you familiar with the late Clarissa Rook?

Joan I'm Lady Bishop's cousin Joan. You must be Inspector O'Reilly.

O'Reilly Yes, I can see the resemblance.

Joan It must have been last Christmas.

O'Reilly When did you last see each other?

O'Reilly and Joan cross each other with a scissors movement

Joan Well, I must go to bed, I'm an archaeologist. You know and I'm excavating the ruins of Highcliff Abbey tomorrow at six a.m. (*She goes up the stairs*)

O'Reilly You'd better be careful, young lady. Those ruins are notoriously unsafe now that the rain has loosened the bricks and cement of the overhanging parapets.

Joan (*coming down*) Don't worry, Inspector.

Pawn enters R with a shovel raised above his head

No, not yet.

Pawn exits

I'll be perfectly safe up there all alone, miles from anywhere. Good-night.

She exits

O'Reilly (*musing*) Highcliff Abbey.

Pawn fails to enter R

(*Meaningfully*) Is that you, Pawn?

Looking for Pawn, he exits L *just as Pawn enters* R *with the shovel. Finding O'Reilly gone, he exits just as O'Reilly enters*

Is that you, Pawn?

Pawn runs on R *with the shovel*

Pawn Now?

Black-out

They exit

There is much banging and crashing, off. Midnight begins to strike. The chimes take forever to reach twelve, during which time absolutely nothing happens. The Lights come up to give a moonlight effect

Régine enters L

Régine Inspectair, Inspectair! Are you 'ere for ze secret rendezvous wiz Régine? Mais non, 'e is not. Brrrr, quelle draught! Oh, ze window is open. (*She closes it*) Zere. Now zat is—'ow you say?—tickety-boo.

Pause. There is a scraping and bumping from behind the painted door

Ah! Oo is zat?

More scraping

No, no, do not come near me!
Pawn (*off*) Hang on. I can't get on.
Régine That's a pretend door.
Pawn (*off*) Why didn't anyone tell me?
Régine You're supposed to be round the other side.
Pawn (*off*) Sorry.

Sound of Pawn running round back of set

(*Off*) Won't be long.
Régine Phew, it is so 'ot in 'ere. I will open ze window. (*She does so and waits, humming the "Marseillaise" and every so often looking over her shoulder towards* L)

Pawn enters through the arch wearing a face mask

Régine hurriedly averts her gaze out of the window. Pawn, unable to see, collides with the armchair, then begins to hit it with a sock full of sand

(*Looking round*) No, over here.

Pawn follows the sound of her voice. When he reaches Régine he hits her violently with the sock

Steady on, dear, for heaven's sake.
Pawn Sorry.

He taps her terribly lightly on the shoulder a couple of times with the sock. Régine moans a little as Pawn tries to push her out of the window—an impossible task

Régine We're never going to do this, dear.
Pawn Can't you lift your leg up?
Régine Get a chair. Get that chair over there.

Pawn hits Régine again with the sock then brings one of the U chairs closer to the window

Get rid of that book.
Pawn It has to stay here. It's terribly important.
Régine Get rid of it.

Pawn throws the book out of the window

Help me up.

Pawn helps Régine on to the chair. She pretends to struggle a little

Now push me. Not that hard!

Régine is helped out of the window. Once safely on the other side she begins to disappear from view—giving a diminishing cry—as if falling from second storey

Pawn Are you all right?
Régine Yes, thank you.

Pawn hits her again

Régine shoots him a malevolent look, sinks beneath the window, then rises stiffly and walks off

Rose (*off*) Did you hear a scream, Violet?
Violet (*off*) 'Appen I did, Rose.

Pawn tries to escape, but finds his coat caught on a nail in the flat

Audrey, as Violet Bishop, appears L pushing Thelma, as Violet's sister, Rose, in a wheelchair. Both are doddering old ladies in dressing-gowns and blankets with strong Yorkshire accents which they sometimes lose. They make little progress on to the stage because the wheelchair brake is on

Rose It seemed to come from in here, like.
Violet Ay.
Rose But there's nowt to be seen.
Violet Nay.
Rose Except that window's open.
Violet Eeeee.
Rose (*forgetting accent*) Are we going in or not?
Violet (*ditto*) Can't move the chair.

Pawn frees himself and runs off up the stairs

Rose Wheel me closer, Violet.

Violet Ay, I will.

Rose I think I can see summat in t' flowerbed.

Violet Eeeee.

Rose Ay, it's Régine the French maid.

Violet Nay.

Rose She's dead, Violet.

Violet By gum!

Rose The brake's on, you idiot.

Violet Oh, I never thought of that. (*She takes the brake off and wheels the wheelchair straight into one of the other chairs*)

Rose Watch where you're going! (*She picks up the chair and hands it to Violet*)

O'Reilly enters L and switches on the standard lamp

Pause. Violet hands O'Reilly the chair. The Lights come up full

O'Reilly Are you Lady Bishop's spinster aunts? (*He passes the chair out through the arch*)

Violet Ay, we're both right frail and we came downstairs to sup cocoa little expecting the hideous sight of a bleeding corpse crushed in the mangled remains of . . . One of my contact lenses has dropped out.

O'Reilly Régine! (*He moves to the window*)

Violet No! Don't move!

O'Reilly The second victim.

Rose What shall we do?

Violet Well, if you can just feel around the floor in this area because it must be here somewhere . . .

O'Reilly I don't think there's anything we can do tonight. After all, it's a bit chilly out there. So why don't we all go to bed and get a good night's sleep?

Rose You know best, young chap.

Violet No, hang on a sec! This is serious. I let the insurance lapse.

There is a bewildered silence while Violet feels around on the floor

O'Reilly So we're all going to bed then.

Rose Yes, and I'm right looking forward to my cocoa.

O'Reilly What sort of cocoa are you going to have?

Violet (*finding the lens*) There he is, the little devil. Let's hope I've got some Transol.

O'Reilly exits

Black-out. A cock is heard crowing. The Lights come up to give a dawn effect, revealing Rose and Violet trying to exit through the painted door. There is the sound of approaching coconut shells

Mrs Reece enters L as Patricia Bishop, Lady Bishop's young equestrienne niece, who wears jodhpurs and boots. She also carries the same red suitcases which were used earlier

The clip-clopping and other horse sound effects continue long after she has entered. Patricia reacts with dismay at Rose and Violet's obvious presence

Patricia I say! It's a beautiful morning. Is anyone up yet?
Violet (*halfheartedly*) We were just going to bed.

Rose and Violet abandon the wheelchair and exit up the stairs

Pawn enters L

Pawn Miss Patricia, after all these years.
Patricia Is that you, Pawn, lurking in the shadows?
Pawn Yes, miss. I will reveal myself to you.

He switches on the standard lamp and the telephone starts ringing. Pawn considers this, then switches the standard lamp off again. The telephone bell stops. Pawn gingerly switches the standard lamp back on. The telephone rings again and Pawn quickly switches the standard lamp off again. The telephone bell stops. Pawn makes a decision. He switches the standard lamp on. The telephone rings. He crosses to the telephone, picks up the receiver, and the bulb in the standard lamp lights up for the first time. Pawn replaces the receiver and the bulb goes out. Pawn is returning to the standard lamp when Patricia interrupts him

Patricia On second thoughts, Pawn, I'll remember you the way you were.

She dries and Pawn has to mouth her next line. Finally she picks up what she thinks is her cue

Sorry, I'm with you now. (*Suddenly emotional*) Pawn, Pawn, something fearful has happened. I've just ridden like the wind from the ruins of Highcliff Abbey, where Joan is lying dead. She was so beautiful and talented, and one of this country's leading archaeologists, but now she's lying under the remains of St Francis of Assisi. What shall we do? What shall we do? (*She cries*)
Pawn We haven't got to this bit yet.
Patricia What?
Pawn You've just skipped five pages.
Patricia It doesn't matter. (*She cues him*) I think you must be imagining things.
Pawn I think you must be imagining things, Miss Patricia.
Patricia Oh, Pawn, how could I imagine that crumpled, ashen-faced corpse that was once a vibrant wife and mother?
Pawn Pray lower your voice, miss. Someone's coming downstairs and we don't want to alarm them needlessly.

Joan appears at the top of the stairs in digging gear, carrying a trowel

Joan Morning, everybody.
Patricia Morning, Joan.

She does a double-take at Joan, who comes downstairs and crosses L

Joan Wonderful day for a dig, isn't it? Well, must fly. I'm working at the ruins of Highcliff Abbey.

Joan exits L

Patricia and Pawn stare at each other

Patricia (*into the wings*) Black-out?

Black-out

Pawn and Patricia exit, striking the cases. O'Reilly comes on and moves C. *Because of the chunk Patricia has left out, no-one is ready for their next cue*

The Lights come up revealing O'Reilly doing up his flies

Daphne rushes on, adjusting her frock, and goes into a clinch with O'Reilly, leaning back in his arms

Daphne Oh, Lionel, I never dreamed I'd meet anyone like you.

O'Reilly overbalances and they both fall on the floor

You're not like other men.

They recover. During the ensuing conversation, Daphne takes a cigarette, then looks for the table-lighter, which has not been set. She notices it being waved through the window, grabs it and tries surreptitiously to slip it on to the telephone-table, where she "discovers" it. Despite Daphne's efforts, the lighter will not ignite. Daphne smokes the cigarette unlit, blowing out invisible smoke

O'Reilly Perhaps there *is* something the teeniest bit special about me, Daph. I reckon the thing that sets me apart from the other lads is my highly-developed power of deduction.

Daphne You mean you know who's been doing these murders here at grand old Checkmate Manor?

O'Reilly No. But I've found a few clues.

Daphne Crumbs, you must be bright. I'm flummoxed.

O'Reilly Well, you'll have been too busy with your lipstick and powder and other girlish things. But I've been keeping my eyes open. Take a look at this book for instance. (*The book is no longer where he set it. He mimes opening a book and reading it*) Régine, your devilishly attractive French maid—no offence, old girl—tried to draw my attention to it just before she met her maker.

Daphne You mean she was trying to tell you something?

O'Reilly Too true. And this is what: "How to . . . How to . . . (*He's forgotten again*) . . . do something or other In Nine Moves".

Daphne moves to the chess-board before O'Reilly mentions it

And look at this chess-board. Each time someone dies a piece mysteriously disappears. Clarissa Rook was strangled and a rook vanished. Gladys Knight was electrocuted and a knight——

Daphne We didn't have her.

O'Reilly Mmmmm?

Daphne She was in the five pages that got missed out.

O'Reilly Oh. So if my deductions are correct, nine chess-men will be appropriated before the murderer fulfils his grisly task.

Daphne gasps

What's the matter?

Daphne Darling.

O'Reilly What's the matter, darling?

Daphne There were going to be nine beneficiaries coming here tonight for the reading of Daddy's will.

O'Reilly Well, judging from the fact that the two kings are the latest pieces to be taken from the board, I predict that King will be the name of the next two murderers ... victims.

Daphne Oh, this is horrible. Mother's brother-in-law, Colonel King, and his wife, Ruby, are expected at any minute.

A dog barks, off

This will be them now.

They move to the window. There is the sound effect of a car driving away, a gramophone needle scratching on the record, the needle trying to find a different effect and finally the effect of a car approaching. Simultaneously the by now familiar red suitcases edge in and out of the curtains of the arch. The car effect stops

    Felicity, as Colonel King, and Audrey, as Mrs King, enter R *carrying the red suitcases, plus an umbrella and the missing book*

Colonel Daphne, m'girl.

Daphne Nunky! Auntie!

Awkward pause. Finally a dog barks, off

Colonel Down, boy.

The Colonel and Mrs King kiss Daphne

Daphne, let me look at yer.

He slides the book across to O'Reilly. He wonders how the Colonel came by it, but has no further use for it, and throws it out of the window

My, how you've grown. You're a gel trembling on the brink of womanhood now. And I see you've already learned that a combination of face shiner and tawny blusher is just the ticket to set off Revlon's metallic frost eye shadow. Now who's this young feller-me-lad?

Daphne Nunky, Auntie: let me introduce Lionel ... er ... Inspector O'Reilly.

Colonel Inspector, eh? Has there been a murder?

O'Reilly Four.

Colonel (*to Mrs King*) This confirms my worst suspicions. (*To Daphne*) Any chance of a spot of tea?

Daphne Yes, I'll ring for Pawn.

Colonel And I'll take the opportunity to get cleaned up.

Suddenly everyone is on the move. Daphne moves to where the bell-rope used to be and can't find it. O'Reilly takes Mrs King to the armchair, where she sits

Colonel King exits L

O'Reilly Tell me, Mrs King: why, when I mentioned the murders, as I did just a moment ago, did your husband say they confirmed his worst suspicions?

Mrs King Simply this, Inspector: nine of the family had discovered a codling startinald to Sir Regiwill's sill ... (*She snaps her fingers in exasperation*) ... a startling codicil to Sir Reginald's will. Edgar was one of these persons and often said that possession of this information put his life in danger.

O'Reilly What was ... ? (*He picks up the chair down* R *and its back comes away in his hand. He carries both halves over to Mrs King*) What was the nature of this codicil?

Mrs King Edgar never told me.

O'Reilly straddles the chair and pretends to rest his elbows on the chair back while actually gripping it between his knees. Much fumbling ensues

Pawn enters L *with a tray of tea*

Pawn You rang, miss?

Daphne Yes, Pawn. Please take these colonels to the case's room and then serve tea.

Pawn Very good, miss.

He realizes he has brought the tray on too early. He tries to give it to Daphne, but she refuses it. Mrs King offers to take it. During ensuing dialogue she passes O'Reilly a cup. He cannot take it until he gives her the chair back. Simultaneously Pawn picks up the cases. Daphne brings one of the U *chairs and sits next to Mrs King*

O'Reilly I know you will be a brave woman, Mrs King, when I tell you that your husband's life *will* be in danger unless he reveals the codicil.

Struggling with the cases, Pawn barges into O'Reilly causing him to throw the contents of his cup over Mrs King

Mrs King Oh! Oh! Then ask him immediately, Inspector, for here he comes now.

Pawn, on hearing this, charges up the stairs, hurls the cases into the wings and pelts round the back of the set

(*Filling in*) Yes, this is Edgar entering now.

O'Reilly Edgar, your husband?

Mrs King Yes, Edgar, my husband, the colonel, is about to walk in immediately and when he does so we shall see him because he is just coming through the door.

Nothing happens

Come in when you're ready, Edgar!

Colonel (*off*) Yes, I'm coming, I'm coming! Just a bit held up here, but I'm almost there ... I'm just about to come ... and here I am.

The Colonel enters L, panting, and with his false moustache half-hanging off his upper lip

You know it's a damn funny thing, Daph, but I couldn't find the guest cloakroom.

Daphne Second on the right, Nunky, dear.

Colonel Top hole.

Colonel exits L

Mrs King Oh, pish. Now we must wait to ask him the vital question.

O'Reilly There's an equally vital question I could ask of you, Mrs King: who in the family plays *chess*?

Hands (supposedly Pawn's but in fact Mrs Reece's), holding a makeshift tray bearing paper cups, a beer mug, etc., appear through the curtains of the arch

Daphne Yet stay. Here's Pawn with the tea.

Mrs King and O'Reilly realize they should not be drinking tea. O'Reilly tries to put his cup on Mrs King's tray, but at the same moment Mrs King puts the tray on Daphne's lap. O'Reilly hides his cup and saucer inside his jacket

Mrs King Did you remember the Hermesetas, Pawn?

Pawn (*off*) Oops, I have erred, ma'am.

The hands withdraw

Mrs King Men so seldom remember that we are living in the era of the weight-watcher.

O'Reilly We look to you ladies to show us the way. May I ask you again, Mrs King: which of the family are chess-players?

Mrs King All of us, Inspector. And we play to win.

Pawn enters L with the makeshift tea-tray

Pawn Your tea, miss. Will that be all?

Daphne refuses to take a second tray. O'Reilly is trying to pass Pawn the cup he shouldn't have. He takes it, but gives him the tray in return

Daphne Yes, Pawn. But I think Nunky's trying to attract your attention.

A hand (supposedly the Colonel's but in fact Mrs Reece's), holding jingling keys, appears through the curtains of the arch and is then withdrawn

Pawn Is that so, miss? Ah, yes, I have neglected to put the colonel's garage in the car. I will speedily remedy the oversight.

Pawn gives O'Reilly's cup to Mrs King and exits L

O'Reilly passes the tray to Mrs King, and in order to take it she passes his cup back to him

Daphne Weak or strong, Inspector?
O'Reilly (*hiding his cup behind his back*) As it comes, please, Miss Bishop.

Daphne takes the handle of the teapot and it detaches itself

Daphne I think we'll let it brew.
Mrs King Edgar!

Felicity enters dressed as Pawn, but in the character of the Colonel

Pawn Here I am, old stick. Is the char ready?
Daphne What are you doing here, Pawn?
Pawn (*realizing*) I ... er ... just came to ... er ... take away the tea.

He attempts to remove Daphne's tray. Daphne won't let go of it

Daphne Get off.
Pawn Please, Thelma! You've already got one!
Daphne It's not in the script!
Pawn (*giving up*) I mean ... I came to take away ... the cigarette box.

Pawn takes the box off the table and dashes off L

Filling in, Mrs King passes O'Reilly a cup. He takes it. She notices he is trying to pass her the one behind his back, she takes it and gives it to Daphne

Mrs King That was lovely ... I mean ... not for me. Thank you. Is there any coffee?
Pawn (*off*) Colonel, Colonel! Are you there?
Colonel (*off*) Yes, here I am, Pawn.
Pawn (*off*) I think the others are waiting for you, Colonel.
Colonel (*off*) Well, I'm just going in. Won't be another minute.
Pawn (*off*) I hear you've been washing your hands, Colonel.
Colonel (*off*) Yes, that's right, Pawn. Washed me hands. And I had a bath as well. And a sauna. And that's why I've been so long. But now I'm going back in. So it's been nice talking to you.

The Colonel enters in more disarray than usual, with the false moustache on his left cheek

Here I am, old stick. Is the char ready?
Mrs King } (*together*) { Yes, come and have a cup.
Daphne } { No, you've missed it.
O'Reilly Colonel, I must talk to you about a matter of the utmost importance.
Colonel I'll get it.

The telephone rings. The Colonel answers it. Ringing continues. As he talks the Colonel walks around the stage revealing that the telephone wire is not attached to anything

(*Without pausing*) Hello, King here. Oh, it's you. Yes, everything's going according to plan. No, I can't say any more. I'm not alone. What? What's that you say? Hello? Hello? (*He hangs up*) Damn, it's gone dead. Come along, Ruby. We must return to town immediately.

O'Reilly I must advise against that, sir.

Colonel Sorry, old boy. I cannot heed that advice. This is a matter of life and death. Pip pip, Daph. We shall return tonight for the reading of the will.

There is the sound of a car starting up and moving off

The Colonel and Mrs King rush to depart

O'Reilly and Daphne rush to the window and point in opposite directions

Daphne There they go.

O'Reilly Yes, up along the cliff edge.

Daphne They're going too fast!

O'Reilly Yes, they seem to be out of control.

Daphne Oh, no!

O'Reilly Somebody must have tampered with the brakes of their car.

The Colonel enters L

Colonel Sorry, forgot my umbrella.

He picks up the umbrella and exits L

O'Reilly They're heading straight over the cliff.

Daphne (*without feeling*) I can't look.

Black-out

Daphne and O'Reilly exit. Mrs Reece enters, carrying her Fashion Show notes

Mrs Reece Sorry. I'm afraid we've had a little hitch back here. What was supposed to have happened was that the car crashed over the cliff, killing the Colonel and Mrs King. Ha-ha-ha-ha! But the gramophone seized up. Isn't it maddening? Anyway, that was the end of Act I. More or less. So we're going to have the Fashion Show now. Preferably with the lights on. I don't know if that's within the realms of possibility, is it?

The Lights come up full

Ah, hey presto. Well, most of you will know that we've been doing these little Fashion Shows for the past twenty years. And I think it's high time we paid tribute to the lady who's been putting so much effort into them during that time, and that's the head of our dressmaking class, Mrs Cavendish.

Enthusiastic applause and cheers from backstage

Yes, she's really been working her knick ... she's been working tremendously hard this year, and of course it's also Mrs Cavendish who thinks up the themes for our shows. She's so fertile. Last year we went colourfully ethnic as Mrs Cav and her team said, "Hello, ladies of the Third World". And older members will recall one of our most ambitious shows, "Into the Space-age with Crimplene". Well, this year we salute the Townswoman Past, Present and Future. So without further ado let's travel back in time sixty years to the very dawn of the Townswomen's Guild movement and remind ourselves of the way we were.

The record of "I Only Have Eyes For You" plays

Audrey enters in thirties' clothes that bear no resemblance to those described by Mrs Reece

(*Reading from her notes*) I wonder how many ladies can remember attending an AGM dressed like this? Audrey is wearing a suit in aquamarine taffeta made by Mrs Gillhooley. That enchanting blouse in pink crêpe de chine is une création de la maison du Mrs Arbuthnot. And is that a red fox fur draped round Audrey's shoulders? (*She looks up from her notes to Audrey*)

Audrey shakes her head

No, it isn't.

Audrey exits

There is disco music and flashing coloured lights

Felicity enters in a smart two-piece, Thelma follows her wearing a leotard and the pair perform a clumsy mannequin routine, Thelma beginning with laboured exercises

(*Reading from her notes*) Elegance remains a keynote as we present the Townswoman of the Eighties dressed for work and play. For her weekly session at the aerobic class Thelma chooses this stretch nylon leotard from the Attractive Outsize Range.

Felicity steps forward to display her clothes

(*As above*) Felicity on the other hand turns heads at the whist drive in this fetching acrylic bouclé skirt and matching jerkin.

Felicity and Thelma produce Union Jacks and dance together

Clever Felicity made the entire outfit herself, and completes her up-to-date look with an accessory which can only be described as a Farndale original.

Felicity opens the top of her jacket revealing a string vest, which she removes, manipulates and displays as a string shopping bag. Thelma puts some items of shopping inside it

"At last," says Felicity, "*haute couture* at Tesco's checkout is a reality."

Felicity and Thelma exit

Let us now look into our crystal ball and try to predict the fashion for Tomorrow's Townswoman ... (*She holds out her hands for something to be passed to her from the wings*)

The piano accordion appears

Mrs Reece shakes her head

The piano accordion is withdrawn and replaced with a snowstorm globe

(*Taking the globe*) Will elegance still be our aim, or will fashion decree a new mode of dress? We hope you will enjoy our lighthearted prophecy of the Townswoman of the Future!

There are two optional endings for ACT I. Ending A:

Electronic music

Gordon enters in outrageously avant-garde fashion

Hail to thee, Townswoman of the Future! What have you to say to us?
Gordon Refreshments are now on sale in the bar.
Mrs Reece Yes, we're now going to have an interval, so we'll see you again in about ten minutes' time for more mystery——

Black-out

—and excitement. I hadn't quite finished, Adrian.

Mrs Reece and Gordon exit

The House Lights come up. The ladies help serve teas during the interval

---

Ending B:
At theatres with flying space the following ending may be deemed preferable

The record of "Fly Me To The Moon" plays

Smoke fills the stage as a rocket descends. Audrey, Thelma and Felicity enter, twirling coloured torches

Not too much smoke, remember! (*She coughs*) That's enough now, thank you! Henry! People will think there's a fire.
Voice (*off*) The switch has jammed!
Mrs Reece (*coughing*) Henry, turn it off! We're choking out here! (*To the audience*) I'm sorry, it's like a Turkish bath, isn't it?

The rocket lands

Hidden by smoke, Gordon, in outrageously avant-garde fashion, enters the back of the rocket then, as smoke clears, emerges through the door at the front, coughing

Hail to thee, Townswoman of the Future! What have you to say to us?
Gordon Refreshments are now on sale in the bar.

Mrs Reece Yes, we're now going to have an interval, so we'll see you again in about ten minutes' time for more mystery——

Black-out

—and excitement. I hadn't quite finished, Adrian.

They exit and the rocket flies up

The House Lights come up and the ladies help serve teas during the interval

ENTR'ACTE

At the end of the interval Mrs Reece shoos everyone back into the auditorium and then mounts the stage. She has a paper containing the Quiz questions

Mrs Reece (*if alternative ending has been used*) Now did you all enjoy our rocket at the end of Act One? Wasn't it magnificent? I know you'll find this hard to believe, but it used to be my immersion heater. (*Otherwise*) Right now! It's Quiz time. Time to get your thinking caps on. We're going to give away a prize, I think. Are we? Yes. Yes, we are. I wasn't quite sure because Woolworth's was closed this afternoon. But we managed to find a bijou nouveauté, so I hope you've still got those little slips that were inside your programmes. Have you? They're for your answers, you see. So if you've lost them we shall be in a bit of a pickle. As we were last night. Oh, you've got yours. Everyone else equipped with a slip? Could I see them waving in the air just to make sure? Oh, yes, that's quite a satisfactory turnout, isn't it? So off we go. There are three questions and each one has got a choice of three answers: (a), (b), or (c). And you just ring what you think is the correct one. All right? So here's the first question, and I think the ladies are going to make light work of this one: in the recipe for lemon soufflé, how many eggs were used? Was it (a) two, (b) four, or (c) ten? Oh, look at these frowns on the gentlemen's faces! This is a complete mystery to you, isn't it? Never mind, we've got a gentlemen's question coming up next. I want you to describe the butler's tool. He had it in his hand when he was over here. Do you remember? It wasn't that funny, was it? Well, anyway, question two is: was the butler's tool (a) a fork, (b) a spade, or (c) a chainsaw? Don't you go telling him, that lady there! There's no satisfaction in cribbing, is there? Everyone ready for question three? Very well, this is question three: which of the characters—and this is a tricky one so think carefully—which of the characters has made a deliberate mistake? Was it (a) Pawn the butler, (b) Lady Doreen Bishop, or (c) Gladys Knight? That's quite a poser, isn't it? But I expect we've got one or two brainboxes here tonight. I must say I saw some frightfully studious folk earlier on. I thought, "Good heavens, what are they doing here?" Anyway do write your name where it says "name" and then pass all the billet-doux along to this end of the rows, and with any luck there should be somebody coming in with a receptacle for them.

Gordon enters the auditorium and passes down the aisle with a bucket, collecting slips

Oh, yes, there he is. It's Gordon. Isn't he a busy bee? Pass them along there. Gordon, dear, did I ask you if you were giving Audrey a lift back to (*name of inaccessible town*)?

Gordon Not now.

Mrs Reece No, not now. After the play.

Gordon nods

Because my car's absolutely chock-a-bloc what with (*names of two local celebrities*).

Gordon Yes, all right.

Mrs Reece That's such a help.

Felicity appears on stage

Felicity Gordon, could you hurry up with the bucket? Mrs Gillhooley's feeling a bit queasy.

Felicity exits

Gordon hurriedly collects remaining slips

Mrs Reece Well, answers later on, but right now I leave you to enjoy the second half of our play.

Felicity appears

Felicity Gordon.

Gordon Yes?

Felicity It's too late.

All exit

The House Lights go down

ACT II

The Lights come up on stage to reveal Violet in the wheelchair, and Rose behind it

Rose Violet, Violet, summat right g . . .

They realize their error and change places

Violet, Violet, summat right gradely's 'appened. Colonel and t' wife are dead.
Violet Eeeee.
Rose You know what this means, don't you?
Violet Nay.
Rose More brass for us!

Both cackle and rub their hands

Well, let's . . .

Violet is still cackling so Rose waits for her to finish

Well, let's stroll round t' garden afore supper.
Violet Shall we take t' lift to t' ground floor?
Rose Ay, same as always. Open t' gates, Vi.

Violet wheels Rose off L

There is the sound effect of lift gates opening, then screams. The Lights fade to Black-out

Pawn enters L, *carrying one red suitcase and switches on the standard lamp. Pause*

The Lights come up full to illuminate the entire stage

Pawn goes to the window and starts drawing the curtains. One draws normally but the other sticks and rips in half as he tries to tug it. He throws the piece of material out of the window

Mrs Reece, as Lady Bishop's extrovert sister Letitia, enters L. *She wears a large cloak and wide-brimmed hat and carries a cigarette holder and the second red suitcase*

Letitia Pawn, darling! (*She drops her case on his foot*) It's been an absolute age since I saw you. I've been rushing from Rome to Hollywood appearing in some of the world's most expensive films, and now here I am back at chilly old Checkmate Manor to see if Reggie's left me any moolah. What have I missed?

Pawn Seven murders, madam.

Letitia Anyone I know?

Pawn No. I mean yes. Most of your relatives.

Letitia Oh, pshaw. They're no loss. What about my vile sister, Doreen, the so-called Lady Bishop. Is she among the victims?

Pawn Oh dearie me, no, madam. Her ladyship is alive and well and about to join us if these old ears do not deceive me.

Letitia Oh, what a bore. I wonder what sort of grand entrance she'll make tonight?

The flat with the painted door shakes violently then Doreen's hand bursts through the canvas. Pawn exits L

Doreen, dear.

Letitia and Doreen shake hands. Doreen's hand then feels round the canvas in search of the non-existent handle

You're looking as radiant as always. Why haven't you kept in touch?

Doreen (*off*) I felt something had come between us.

Letitia You're damn right. You stole Reggie, turned me into an alcoholic, and melted down my Tupperware.

Doreen appears at the top of the stairs

Doreen (*moving down the stairs*) Don't be bitter, Letitia.

Letitia I warned you never to mention my operation. Haven't I paid enough?

Doreen Why don't you lie down?

Letitia No! I'm going to lie down.

Doreen Sorry. Would you like a drink?

Letitia But when the will is read tonight, I shall have the last laugh.

Doreen I haven't a clue what I say now.

Letitia I want to see you suffer, Doreen. You're going to suffer like you made me suffer when you ironed out my pleated skirt. Just you wait. Ha-ha-ha-ha! (*She turns to go up the stairs then turns back*) Did I say the bit about the Tia Maria?

Doreen I don't know.

Daphne enters L

Daphne Mother, Pawn said that Aunt Letitia had arrived. Is she here?

Doreen No, she's having a lie down.

Letitia Tell Pawn to——

Daphne But I must speak to her. The inspector says she might be in great danger.

Doreen She'll be asleep now.

Letitia Tell Pawn to bring me a Tia Maria. Ow! Don't pinch, Thelma. It's very spiteful.

Letitia exits

Daphne But see here, Mother. Another bishop is missing from the board!

Doreen I fail to see the significance of that. Now don't be an old fusspot, there's a dear. The solicitor will be arriving any minute now to read the will so I must ... er ... something about going to the kitchen.

Doreen exits

Daphne stands musing by the chess-board

O'Reilly enters L and starts to creep over to her

Daphne is blatantly aware of his presence and she gets progressively slower in her delivery in order to time her last word with O'Reilly putting his hands on her shoulders

Daphne Why won't anyone believe me? I know there's going to be another murder here before midnight. The proof's right here on this board. Perhaps there are more clues to be found here. Like ... the ... identity of ... the ... killer.

O'Reilly puts his hands on her shoulders and she turns to him without the slightest hint of surprise

Lionel, you scared me half to death.

O'Reilly Sorry, old girl. I just wanted to tell you that you shouldn't be wandering about alone tonight.

Daphne Oh, Lionel, to hear you say that, one would assume you really cared about me.

O'Reilly I do, and heaps too. In fact you mean more than the whole world to me, Deirdre ... Daphne.

Daphne I think I'm walking on air. My head's in the clouds and I'm floating light as a feather.

O'Reilly Well, come back down to earth and tell me if you'll be my steady girl.

Daphne Oh, yes, Lionel, yes, yes.

There is an embarrassed embrace

This could be a passport to true happiness.

This is a cue for song, but there is a long delay before the intro to "I Could Be Happy With You" is heard. O'Reilly moves down R, Daphne down L. They mime to the voices on the record, but after the first couple of lines, O'Reilly gives up and Daphne mimes to both the male and female parts. During the middle eight they are passed hats and canes, and execute some extremely simple and naff dance movements

Towards the end of the song, Pawn brings on a pink cardboard heart

Ostensibly O'Reilly and Daphne kiss behind it, but when Pawn drops it, they are revealed to be looking away from each other

Pawn retreats off L

O'Reilly is grappling with hats, canes and cardboard heart

Mrs Reece, as Mr Goodbody, a city gent, enters L

Goodbody Upon my soul!

Daphne Who are you?

Goodbody I, madam, am Mr . . . (*He has forgotten*)

Daphne Goodbody.

Goodbody I am Mr Goodbody of Goodbody, Goodbody and Goodbody, solitioners and commissitors for oaths. On the stroke of midnight I intend to read the last will and testament of the late Sir Reginald Bishop.

Daphne Oh, yes, Mr Goodbody. We've been expecting you. Can I take your luggage?

Goodbody I couldn't find it.

Daphne What?

O'Reilly (*pointing* C *to the red suitcase*) It's there.

Goodbody Ah, yes indeed. (*He picks up the case*) Well . . . shall we go down to dinner?

Doreen hurries in L

Doreen Would everybody like to come down to dinner?

Felicity (*off*) Poison! Poison! Aaarrgghh! I've been poisoned!

Felicity, totally enveloped in Letitia's cloak and hat, appears at the top of the stairs

(*Staggering down the stairs*) Poison! Poison! I've been poisoned! (*She finishes sitting carefully in the armchair*)

Doreen What's happened?

O'Reilly She's been poisoned.

Daphne Oh, I do hope it's nothing serious.

A dog barks, off

Felicity Down b——

Black-out

All exit

There is the sound effect of a car going over a cliff and the Lights come up

Goodbody pokes his head round a flat

Goodbody Sorry. That was the car crash from the first half. Sorry.

He disappears. O'Reilly, Doreen, Daphne and Goodbody enter L, *wiping their lips with napkins. Pawn enters* L *with a silver tray of empty port glasses plus a tennis ball and begins serving everyone*

O'Reilly What a positively delightful meal, Lady Bishop.

Doreen It was nothing.

O'Reilly But surely those crab balls must have taken an age to prepare.

Doreen Oddly enough they're quick and easy as well as being economical.

O'Reilly is taken aback by the tennis ball left on the tray

Pawn Couldn't find the other glass.

O'Reilly reluctantly takes the ball. Pawn goes up c *to Daphne and Goodbody. O'Reilly chinks his ball against Doreen's glass and then raises the ball to his lips*

Doreen After chopping six ounces of crabmeat, mix it with three ounces of breadcrumbs, some seasoning, one egg yolk and a teaspoon of lemon juice. Beat the mixture until thick and then shape it into balls. Coat each ball with egg white and browned breadcrumbs, and then fry them for five to six minutes until golden brown. You can serve them hot or cold.

O'Reilly Mmmm. And how many balls will I end up with?

Doreen Well, Inspector, if you're having six policemen round for dinner, they should have two balls each.

O'Reilly That sounds ideal.

Doreen and O'Reilly hang on to each other sniggering over the preceding "double entendre". Midnight strikes—another agonizingly long process. Pawn notices that the light reflected off his tray can be moved around the audience's faces. He is greatly enjoying this trick until Goodbody sees the moving light, traces its source, and tells Pawn off. Goodbody falls into conversation with Daphne. Pawn takes the opportunity to play with the tray again. This time Daphne stops him. The chimes cease

Goodbody Well, of course, I wouldn't have seen it if I hadn't been looking out of the window at that precise time, but there, right in front of my eyes, without an iota of shame, was (*person well-known to or present in audience*) bending over his ... has it finished?

Daphne Yes.

Goodbody Oh. (*He comes down* c) Midnight has struck. Are all the beneficiaries present?

Doreen All except my equestrienne niece, Patricia, who is at this moment galloping homeward.

Goodbody Someone will have to give her a message. Shall we convene?

There is the interminably complex business of everyone bringing chairs into a semi-circle c

Goodbody brings the broken chair UR *and exits* L

Daphne places UL *chair* DL *and sits*

Pawn moves the armchair UC, *places* UR *chair* L *of Daphne, and exits* L

Doreen exits L, *enters, replaces the armchair and sits*

O'Reilly exits L, *enters with a chair, places it* R *of the armchair and sits*

Daphne replaces the chair on her L UL

Goodbody takes Daphne's chair off R

O'Reilly replaces the broken chair DR. *Doreen takes O'Reilly's chair and places it far* L. *Daphne finds her chair missing, moves the armchair into its place and sits*

Pawn enters L with chair and places it R of Daphne

O'Reilly finds his chair missing, fetches the DL chair, places it and sits

Goodbody enters R, replaces the broken chair and exits R

Daphne takes the chair on her right off L and enters

Doreen replaces the armchair C and sits. Pawn places the DL chair R of the armchair. O'Reilly replaces the broken chair DR, returns to his chair and sits

Goodbody enters R with a chair and places it R of O'Reilly

Daphne finds the armchair missing, fetches the UL chair, places it DL and sits. Doreen takes the chair on her right and places it far L

Pawn moves the armchair UC and exits R

O'Reilly takes the chair on his right and exits R with it

Goodbody places the broken chair R of Daphne

Daphne moves the broken chair far R and exits R

Doreen replaces the armchair DC and sits

Pawn enters R with a chair and places it R of the armchair

O'Reilly enters R, takes his chair and exits R with it

Goodbody takes the far L chair and exits L with it

Pawn takes the broken chair off R

Doreen takes the chair on her right off L

Goodbody enters L, takes Daphne's chair and exits L with it

The stage is now empty apart from the armchair

Everybody enters and reacts with surprise at the empty stage

Goodbody and Daphne both make for the armchair. Daphne manages to wedge herself in by pinching Goodbody, who slides with bad grace on to the arm

Seeing the tussle over the armchair, Pawn exits and re-enters with the broken chair

Pawn Here you are, Mrs Reece. (*He places the broken chair L of the armchair*)

Goodbody slides across on to it. Pawn moves away from the chair, accidentally removing its back. Goodbody leans back and falls on the floor. General bumbling as he is helped to his feet. He then begins searching his clothing while muttering inaudibly

Daphne (*patronizingly*) We're finding it difficult to hear you, Mr Goodbody.
Goodbody I've forgotten the bloody will!

Goodbody marches off L

A gunshot is heard, off

Goodbody returns

(*Into the wings*) Not now! (*He sits down and opens a paper*)

Doreen and O'Reilly bend their knees, pretending to sit on chairs. This causes them some discomfort

I must say this is a most unorthodox document. However, Sir Reginald was quite specific about his wishes, which I will now reveal unto you: "I, Reginald Bishop, being of sound mind and body, do hereby direct that my rambling estate and huge fortune shall be divided equally between my surviving relatives and, that in the unlikely event of everyone dying, absolutely everything shall go to my horse-loving niece, Patricia."

Daphne ⎫
O'Reilly ⎭ (*together*) Patricia? Good heavens, this is astounding!

Doreen This surely can——
O'Reilly Amazing.
Doreen This surely can——
Daphne Incredible.
Doreen This surely can——
O'Reilly Astonishing. Sorry.

Pause. Doreen checks to see whether anyone else is going to speak

Doreen (*very quickly*) This surely cannot be, dear Mr Goodbody. For if it be true, it would seem to suggest that the person with the strongest motive for killing us all is kind-hearted Patricia, friend of the animals.
O'Reilly May I examine the document, Mr Goodbody?
Goodbody (*starting to remove his clothes*) I'm afraid not. It's secret. And now, having discharged my duty, I must bid you good-night.

Goodbody exits L *with his hat and tie in his hand and his trousers round his ankles*

Doreen Pawn, show Mr Goodbody the door.

Pawn, miles away, looks blankly at Doreen

Door.
Pawn (*looking at the door*) What about it?
Doreen Show Mr Goodbody the door.
Pawn Mr Goodbody! Would you like to have a look at the door?

Pawn exits

Doreen Well! When Patricia returns home she will get the sharp edge of *my* tongue.

The Lights fade to Black-out. There is the sound of approaching coconut shells, which speed up to a silly rate before slowing again. The Lights come up revealing O'Reilly, Doreen and Daphne asleep in various unnatural postures

Mrs Reece, as Patricia, enters L, *pulling on riding boots*

Patricia I say! Have I missed the reading of the will? Oh, corks. They're all asleep.

Pawn enters L *with a brown paper parcel which has a very obvious, thick, black cable running from it to the wings*

Pawn Begging your pardon, miss: this parcel has just been delivered for you. (*He places the parcel on the floor*)

Patricia How super. One so rarely receives a postal delivery at two o'clock in the morning.

Pawn Nothing is too much trouble for an artistocrat such as yourself, miss.

Pawn exits L *with his fingers in his ears*

The others cringe in anticipation

Patricia What can it be?

The parcel fails to explode

A pause, then Pawn appears through the curtained arch, clicking a non-operative switch

Pawn Bang.

Pawn exits

Patricia screams and falls to the floor. In doing so, her riding hat falls off. She has time to retrieve it and put it back on her head before expiring

O'Reilly Look after your mother, Daphne. The Checkmate Manor monster has struck again in order to claim Patricia, who could have gone on to become Horsewoman of the Year.

Daphne Patricia? But this means she's not the killer.

O'Reilly That's right, old girl. The beast is still in our midst.

Daphne moves to get out of the armchair, and Doreen moves to take her place. A dog barks, off. Daphne resumes her position, and Doreen hers. At the end of the effect Daphne gets up and goes to the window, and Doreen usurps her seat

Daphne Look at old Rover bounding around down there. I'm sure he's trying to tell us who the murderer is.

O'Reilly joins Daphne at the window and they exchange places

O'Reilly Hmmm. I wonder . . .

A dog yelps, off

Daphne Rover!

Pawn enters carrying a heavy spanner and with a dog lead dangling out of his pocket

Pawn More bad news, milady: obedient old Rover has fetched his last pair of slippers.

Doreen Oh, Pawn, no. Not dead? Not harmless old Rover?

Pawn (*nodding*) Quite suddenly. (*He slaps the spanner into the palm of his hand*)

O'Reilly Thanks for the news, Pawn. Now please remove ... er ... what's her name, who is also no longer alive, and then cut along back here to the drawing-room.

Pawn As you wish, sir.

He attempts to push Patricia off by her feet, fails, and stops for advice when Patricia is folded up with her feet behind her head

What shall I do?

Doreen Oh, just leave her.

Pawn exits. Patricia executes a backward roll and follows him off

O'Reilly I see it all now.

Daphne What can you mean?

O'Reilly Lady Bishop, Daphne: I know who the killer is, and I can confidently predict that within five minutes he will expose himself in front of you.

Doreen and Daphne look suitably aghast

As the Lights fade to Black-out the parcel is slowly pulled off stage

Doreen corpses

Doreen, Daphne and O'Reilly exit

The House Lights come up

Mrs Reece enters carrying the Prize, a handbag, and a piece of paper with the Quiz winner's name on it

Mrs Reece Well, at this very exciting juncture, I'm going to prolong the suspense even more because we've now selected the winner of our Murder Mystery quiz. The name's on this piece of paper. But first of all we'd better run through the answers, which I wrote on the back of something or other. (*She hunts in her bag, producing a scrap of paper*) Ah, here we are. Question one: well, we use four eggs in our lemon soufflé. They may do it differently on the Continent, but then we don't live there, do we? Question two: ah yes, now this concerned the nature of the butler's tool. (*She reacts to laughter*) So you're the ones who spoiled your papers, are you? I've got one word to say: cheap. I'm sorry. The correct answer was in fact a spade. And finally it was Lady Doreen Bishop who made tonight's deliberate mistake. I'm sure no-one in her right mind would try to remove tea stains with vinegar. That was really far too easy, wasn't it? Well, so much for that. And now the moment of truth: our winner tonight is (*whoever*).

The winner is invited to join Mrs Reece

Well, you're our super-sleuth tonight, so we've got a little something for you that we think you'll appreciate. It's this game called "Mastermind".

One pound twenty. And just to make it more difficult, we're giving you the one with the rules in Portuguese. (*She presents the prize*) So there you are. Oh! and incidentally: have you worked out whodunit yet? Don't give it away; just yes or no. You know it, do you? Oh, you're too clever for us. Are you at university? (*Or*: Are you doing an Open University course?) Well, you're certainly a bright one, anyway. It's been so nice to meet you. Thank you ever so much. And now let's have that climax we've all been waiting for.

Mrs Reece exits

The House Lights go down and the Lights come up

> *Doreen enters* L, *Daphne enters* R *and both make for the armchair. This time Doreen is quicker, and Daphne is forced to slide on to the chair without a back. Just as she leans absent-mindedly backwards, Pawn bursts in with the chair back*

Pawn Thelma! Don't . . .

Too late. Pawn hides the chair back behind him. Daphne gets to her feet

> *O'Reilly enters*

O'Reilly I expect you're wondering why I asked you here. Well, I'll tell you: one of us in this room is a murderer.

Doreen and Daphne gasp

Don't worry, ladies. It is neither of you. The person we are dealing with is a cunning devil. Not only has he been killing everyone who stood in his path to the Bishop millions, he also drew our attention to his intended victims by leaving cryptic clues on this chess-board. But then he got too clever. He left me a clue as to his own identity by moving his knight to king's bishop three. And from this it was easy to deduce that our murderer devised his cunning plot with . . . (*He dries, fiddling with props while he waits for the line to come*) Our murderer devised his cunning plot with . . . (*He pokes his head through the curtained arch*) Who did our murderer devise his cunning plot with?

Mrs Reece (*off*) Clarissa.

O'Reilly With his sister?

Mrs Reece (*off*) With Clarissa, you idiot!

O'Reilly With Clarissa, you idiot, who was then killed because . . . why?

Mrs Reece (*off*) She wanted too big a piece of the action.

O'Reilly Yes, she wanted too big a piece of the action. Fifi, the French maid, was his mistress . . .

Doreen Régine.

O'Reilly Régine, the French maid, was his mistress—sorry. And she had to die because she knew too much. (*To Pawn*) Who's next?

Pawn The Colonel.

O'Reilly The Colonel wouldn't tell what he knew. So he was killed. But he told . . . (*To Doreen*) Was it the spinsters?

Doreen nods

He told Rose and Violet. And they spilled the beans. And they were killed as well. Letitia ... spilled some more beans ... (*He looks through the torn canvas of the painted door for more help*) Pardon? Er ... white, two sugars. No! Who's next? Oh, yes. Gladys Knight was crucial to the operation because——

Pawn ⎱
Doreen ⎰ (*together*) Gordon.

O'Reilly What?

Pawn ⎱
Doreen ⎰ (*together*) We didn't have her.

O'Reilly (*through the canvas*) We didn't have her. Right. (*Out front*) Mr Goodbody was blackmailed into throwing us off the scent. And then there was ... thingummy ... just now. Only one person could have perpetrated all these crimes.

Pawn moves down C

Daphne You mean ...?

O'Reilly Yes——

Mrs Reece darts on from L *with three hand-written pages of dialogue*

Mrs Reece Going to have to cut in there, dear. Felicity! Giles is on the phone!

Pawn Well, I'll talk to him later!

Mrs Reece No, you've got to come now.

Pawn We've just got to my big bit.

Mrs Reece It's Lucy, dear.

Pawn What about her?

Mrs Reece I couldn't understand what he was saying. He was getting hysterical.

Pawn (*starting to run off; muttering*) The one night I have off, and something happens ...

Pawn exits

Mrs Reece (*to the audience*) Do bear with us, ladies and gentlemen. At times like this a mother's place is with her child. I'm sure you'll agree.

Pawn runs in again, with a gun, and poses

Pawn You'll never take me alive ...

Mrs Reece Give me that, Felicity. We're going to carry on without you.

Pawn But I want to shoot myself!

Mrs Reece Some other time.

Pawn It's not fair!

Mrs Reece Gordon, I've done a bit of rewriting. Could you pass these along, please? (*She hands three pages of dialogue to O'Reilly*)

Pawn It's the only reason I agreed to play Pawn ...

Mrs Reece You can shoot yourself in the next play. Now let's get you to the telephone ...

Mrs Reece bustles Pawn out of the arch

The pages of dialogue are distributed among those on stage and read stiltedly

O'Reilly Only one person could have perpetrated all these crimes.
Daphne You mean ... ?
O'Reilly Yes. (*He turns aimlessly*) Come out from behind that secret panel, Régine.

Mrs Reece bounds in from L as Régine

Régine Oui, c'est moi.
Daphne (*vividly unimpressed*) But, Régine, you're dead.
O'Reilly No, she was pretending.
Doreen Tell us the whole story, Inspector.
O'Reilly Why don't we let Régine tell us in her own words?
Daphne (*looking up from paper; under her breath*) Must we?
Régine Ooh-la-la, I 'ave been so clever. I blackmail Monsieur Goodbody not to reveal secret codicil of will, which say zat I get all ze money if everyone die. I kill everyone, disguised as Pawn ze butler, 'oo try to foil my plan by pushing me out of ze window. But I save myself by clinging to ze window sill. And zen I 'ide behind ze secret panel.
Doreen But why should my husband leave his money to a common serving girl?
Régine Because we were 'aving an affair.
Doreen (*expressionlessly*) No, no, I cannot believe it. Even though I have lost all my youth and beauty, Reginald loved me and would never leave me for a ... (*with incredulity*) ... beautiful young girl with bags of personality!
Régine (*prompting*) And the body of a Greek goddess.
Doreen (*to keep the peace*) And the body of a Greek goddess.
Daphne I'm afraid you'll have to face facts, Mother: Régine may be a mass murderer, but ... she's easily the most attractive woman in this room?

The indignity of having to speak these lines is too much for her and Daphne stalks off R

O'Reilly Aren't you ashamed of yourself for killing all these people?
Régine No, I'm glad, I tell you, glad, glad, glad.
O'Reilly I'm afraid you'll have to come along with me.
Régine You'll never take me alive. (*She picks up the revolver*)
O'Reilly Look out, she's got a gnu.
Régine Gun!
O'Reilly A gun.
Régine I go to join my beloved Reggie in a far, far better place. Au revoir. (*She points revolver at her head and closes her eyes, but the trigger is too stiff to pull. She laughs nervously*) I think it could do with a drop of oil.

She holds out the revolver to O'Reilly. He takes a step towards her and the revolver goes off. Régine screams and goes into the death scene she's planned. The climax to the "1812 Overture" plays. Régine collapses into O'Reilly's arms, but he is not ready for her. She staggers over to the stairs, collapses there, but then gets up again and goes to the window where she indulges in further death scene antics, bringing down the remaining curtain

Régine stumbles through the arch, but a moment later bursts back on again and clings to the standard lamp for support

With her last gasp, she totters to the armchair and flings herself across Doreen's lap. Doreen distastefully pushes her to the floor. O'Reilly applauds spontaneously

Black-out. The Lights come up again revealing no-one in the correct places for the line-up

There are ragged curtain calls during which Mrs Reece and Thelma constantly jostle for the centre position, and Felicity appears occasionally while struggling into her raincoat

The House Lights come up as——

—the CURTAIN *falls*

FURNITURE AND PROPERTY LIST

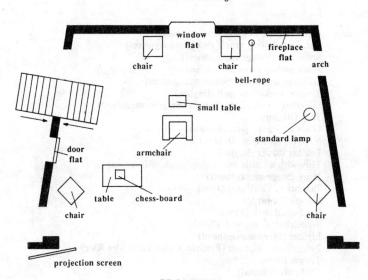

exterior backing

window flat

chair

chair

fireplace flat

arch

bell-rope

small table

standard lamp

armchair

door flat

table

chess-board

chair

chair

projection screen

PROLOGUE

Front of house:
Projection screen
Stand or table. *On it:* 8mm movie projector with film (practical—set out of focus)

On stage:
Fireplace flat with "The Laughing Cavalier" hanging above mantelpiece (collapsible). *At the back:* pieces of paper with cues
Window flat (practical). *Above window:* pelmet (collapsible). Either side of window: curtains (collapsible), one of which rips in half
Curtained arch
Small table with detachable leg. *On it:* chess-board and pieces
Set of stairs with detachable bannister
4 upright chairs, one with detachable back
Armchair. *Under it:* telephone
Small table hidden behind armchair. *On it:* magazines, cigarette box, ashtray, sewing-box with collapsible base containing embroidery with needle and thread, cotton etc.
Bell-rope (detachable)
Standard lamp

Off stage: Programmes containing slips of paper for Murder Mystery Quiz **(Mrs Reece** and **Thelma)**
Packets of fudge **(Mrs Reece** and **Thelma)**
Notes **(Mrs Reece)**

Personal: **Thelma:** "Miss Farndale 1988" sash

ACT I

On stage: As before

Off stage: Piano accordion **(Stage-management)**
Candlestick with candle **(Stage-management)**
Snowflakes **(Stage-management)**
Black bishop chess-piece **(Clarissa)**
Dustpan and brush **(Stage-management)**
Tennis racquet and ball **(Daphne)**
Different coloured tennis balls **(Stage-management)**
Tray **(Régine)**
Glass of orange juice **(Régine)**
Napkins **(O'Reilly, Daphne)**
Feather duster **(Régine)**
Tray with a bottle and a glass stuck to it **(Pawn)**
Book **(Stage-management)**
2 empty red suitcases **(Joan)**
Shovel **(Pawn)**
Sand-filled sock **(Pawn)**
Wheelchair **(Rose** and **Violet)**
Lighter **(Stage-management)**
2 empty red suitcases **(Patricia, Colonel** and **Mrs King)**
Trowel **(Joan)**
Umbrella **(Colonel)**
Book **(Colonel)**
Tea-tray. *On it:* cups, saucers, teapot with detachable handle **(Pawn)**
Tea-tray. *On it:* paper cups, beer mug **(Mrs Reece)**
Bunch of keys **(Mrs Reece)**
Fashion Show notes **(Mrs Reece)**
Items of shopping **(Stage-management)**
Piano accordion **(Stage-management)**
Snowstorm globe **(Stage-management)**
Rocket (for alternative ending to ACT I) **(Stage-management)**
Coloured torches **(Audrey, Thelma** and **Felicity)**

Personal: **Daphne:** smelling salts in pocket
Joan: spectacles
Pawn: face mask
Colonel: false moustache
Felicity: Union Jack in pocket
Thelma: Union Jack in pocket

ENTR'ACTE

On stage: As before

Off stage: List of Quiz questions **(Mrs Reece)**
Bucket **(Gordon)**

ACT II

On stage: As before

Off stage: 1 empty red suitcase **(Pawn)**
Cigarette holder **(Letitia)**
1 empty suitcase **(Letitia)**
2 hats and canes **(O'Reilly, Daphne)**
Pink cardboard heart **(Pawn)**
Napkins **(O'Reilly, Doreen, Daphne, Goodbody)**
Tray of port, glasses and tennis ball **(Pawn)**
Chair **(O'Reilly)**
Paper **(Goodbody)**
Brown paper parcel with thick black cable **(Pawn)**
Heavy spanner **(Pawn)**
Quiz prize, paper with Quiz winner's name **(Mrs Reece)**
3 pages of dialogue **(Mrs Reece)**
Revolver **(Pawn)**

Personal: **Pawn:** dog lead dangling from pocket
Mrs Reece: handbag. *In it.* Quiz answers

LIGHTING PLOT

Practical fittings required: standard lamp

Interior. Same scene throughout

PROLOGUE

To open: House Lights on

| Cue 1 | Fanfare | (Page 1) |
| | *House Lights down, bring up front stage lighting* | |

| Cue 2 | **Mrs Reece:** "All right, Thelma." | (Page 2) |
| | *Black-out* | |

| Cue 3 | **Thelma:** "Anyone got some Sellotape?" | (Page 2) |
| | *House Lights up* | |

| Cue 4 | **Audrey** runs off | (Page 3) |
| | *House Lights down* | |

ACT I

To open: Flashes of lightning. Bright sunlight from window

| Cue 5 | **Clarissa** buttons up her nightgown | (Page 4) |
| | *Bring up dim lighting* | |

| Cue 6 | **Clarissa** clicks light switch | (Page 4) |
| | *Black-out* | |

| Cue 7 | **Clarissa:** ". . . to be on now." | (Page 4) |
| | *Bring up full general lighting* | |

| Cue 8 | **Clarissa** clicks switch (2nd time) | (Page 4) |
| | *Imperfect black-out* | |

| Cue 9 | **Clarissa** clicks switch (3rd time) | (Page 4) |
| | *Bring up full general lighting* | |

| Cue 10 | **Clarissa** falls to the floor | (Page 5) |
| | *Imperfect black-out* | |

| Cue 11 | As **Clarissa** replaces the pelmet and curtains | (Page 5) |
| | *Bring up full general lighting* | |

| Cue 12 | **Pawn:** "Down, boy." | (Page 11) |
| | *Black-out, then almost immediately bring up full lighting* | |

| Cue 13 | **Pawn:** "Now?" | (Page 15) |
| | *Black-out* | |

ENTR'ACTE

To open: Full general lighting

ACT II

To open: Full general lighting

| *Cue* 31 | **Pawn** enters | (Page 33) |
| | *Increase lighting on* **Pawn** | |

| *Cue* 32 | **Doreen:** "... edge of *my* tongue." | (Page36) |
| | *Fade to Black-out. Pause, then bring up full general lighting* | |

| *Cue* 33 | **Doreen** and **Daphne** look aghast | (Page 38) |
| | *Fade slowly to Black-out. Pause, then bring up House Lights* | |

| *Cue* 34 | **Mrs Reece** exits through auditorium door | (Page 39) |
| | *Fade House Lights and when ready bring up full general lighting* | |

| *Cue* 35 | **Doreen** pushes **Régine** to the floor | (Page 42) |
| | *Black-out, then bring up full general lighting* | |

| *Cue* 36 | When curtain calls have finished | (Page 42) |
| | *House Lights go up* | |

EFFECTS PLOT

Please read the notice on page 51 concerning the use of copyright music and commercial recordings

PROLOGUE

Cue 1   As the audience arrive   (Page 1)
         A selection of music ending with a fanfare

ACT I

Cue 2   To open   (Page 4)
         Thunder

Cue 3   **Clarissa** buttons her nightgown   (Page 4)
         Knocking

Cue 4   **Clarissa:** "... remote country house by the sea."   (Page 4)
         Knocking

Cue 5   **Clarissa** exits R   (Page 4)
         Knocking

Cue 6   **Doreen:** "Hist."   (Page 7)
         Deafening sound

Cue 7   **Régine** runs from L to R behind the window   (Page 8)
         Knocking

Cue 8   **Doreen:** "... police car approaching."   (Page 9)
         Vast traffic noise: horns blowing, juggernauts, newsvendors' cries
         etc. with police siren eventually heard. Snap off traffic effect
         and then bring up knocking

Cue 9   **Pawn:** "Dinner is served, milady."   (Page 11)
         Gong sounded

Cue 10   **Pawn:** "Be about your business, my girl."   (Page 11)
         Dog barks

Cue 11   During Black-out   (Page 15)
         Banging and crashing noises followed by slow midnight chimes

Cue 12   Black-out   (Page 17)
         Cock crows

Cue 13   Dawn light effect comes up   (Page 17)
         Clip-clop effect of coconut shells growing louder interspersed with
         *horse effects. Continue for some time after **Patricia's** entrance*

Cue 14	**Pawn** switches standard lamp on and off 3 times in sequence *Telephone rings and stops 3 times in sequence as text*	(Page 18)
Cue 15	**Daphne:** "... at any minute." *Dog barks*	(Page 20)
Cue 16	**Daphne** and **O'Reilly** move to the window *Effect of recording of car driving away, needle scratching on* *record, trying to find a different effect and finally car approaching*	(Page 20)
Cue 17	**Daphne:** "Nunky! Auntie!" *Pause followed by dog bark*	(Page 20)
Cue 18	**Colonel:** "I'll get it." *Telephone rings and continues after* **Colonel** *speaks*	(Page 24)
Cue 19	**Colonel:** "... for the reading of the will." *Car starts up and moves off. Continue car noise*	(Page 24)
Cue 20	**Daphne:** "I can't look." *Snap off car effect*	(Page 24)
Cue 21	**Mrs Reece:** "... the way we were." *Record of "I Only Have Eyes For You"*	(Page 25)
Cue 22	**Audrey** exits *Disco music*	(Page 25)
Cue 23	**Felicity** and **Thelma** exit *Snap off disco music*	(Page 25)
Cue 24	**Mrs Reece:** "... the Townswoman of the Future." *Electronic music or record of "Fly Me To The Moon" for* *alternative ending to ACT I*	(Page 26)
Cue 24A	Record of "Fly Me To The Moon" plays *Smoke effect*	(Page 26)

ENTR'ACTE

No cues

ACT II

Cue 25	**Violet** wheels **Rose** off L *Sound of lift gates opening and screams*	(Page 30)
Cue 26	**Daphne:** "... passport to true happiness." *A pause, then record of "I Could Be Happy With You"*	(Page 32)
Cue 27	**Daphne:** "... it's nothing serious." *Dog barks*	(Page 33)
Cue 28	Black-out *Effect of a car going over a cliff*	(Page 33)

MADE AND PRINTED IN GREAT BRITAIN BY
LATIMER TREND & COMPANY LTD PLYMOUTH

MADE IN ENGLAND